How To Draw Anime Faces

A Step by Step Guide

Printed in the United States of America

9798698379171

INSTRUCTIONS

Here you will find the basic steps necessary to replicate the faces found throughout this book.

 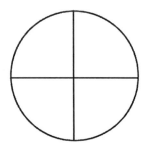

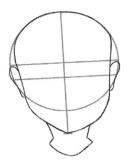

Every face starts out with a basic circle.

The second step is where we add to the circle by giving it a neck and jawline.

In the third step we begin to add the first set of details such as the hair.

In the fourth step we add the eyes, eyebrows, nose and other facial features. We also begin erasing lines that are no longer necessary.

Finally, in the fifth step we erase any lines no longer necessary and add shading to select areas of the face to give it greater depth.

GRAPHING PAPER

OPPOSITE EACH GUIDE YOU WILL FIND A BLANK SHEET OF OF 4X4 GRAPH PAPER. BY FOCUSING IN ON THE GRIDS YOU CAN BETTER PINPOINT AND EMULATE THE ART FEATURED IN THE GUIDES.

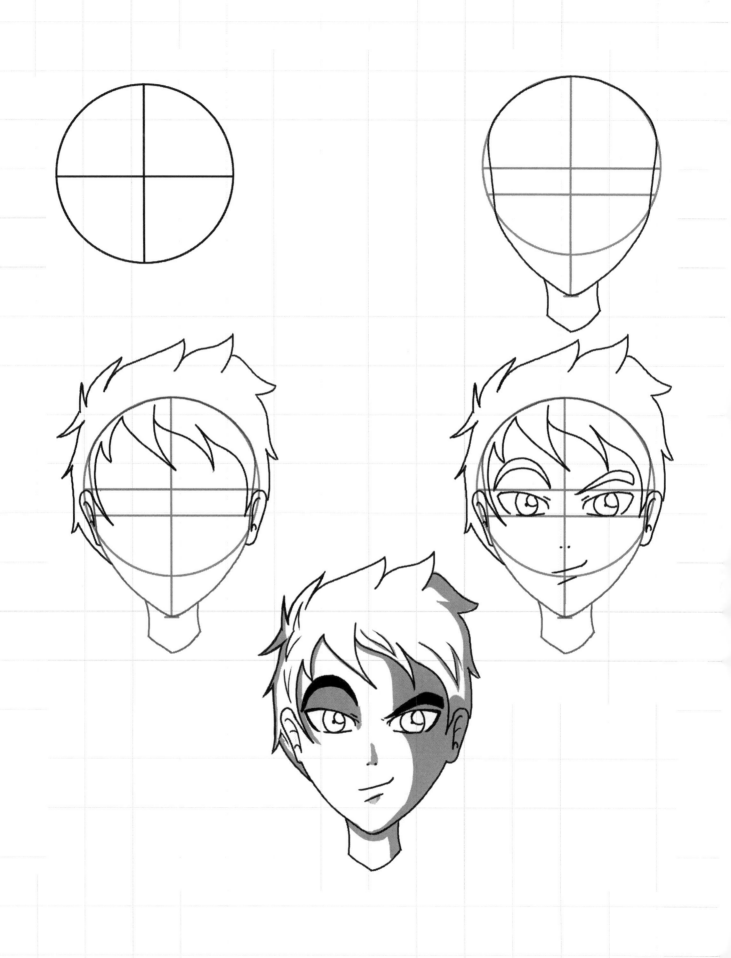

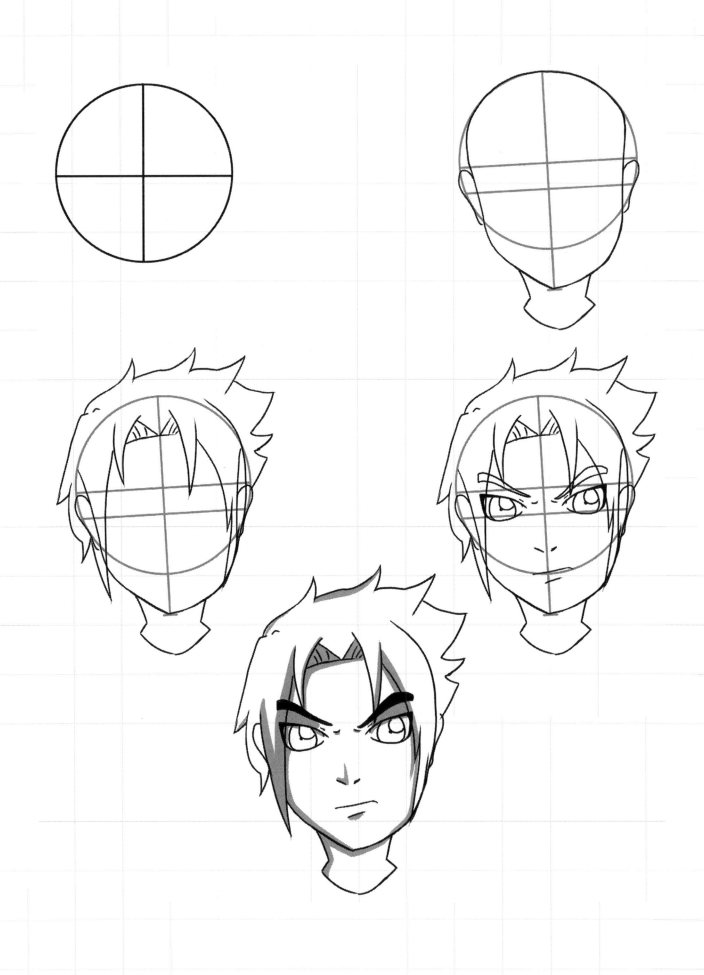

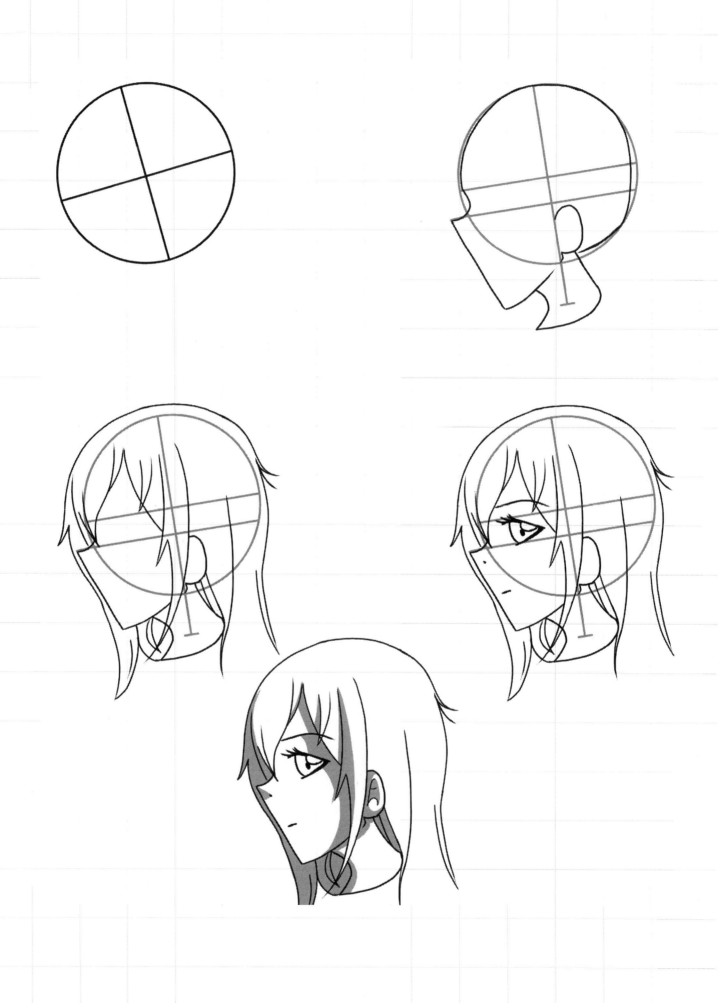

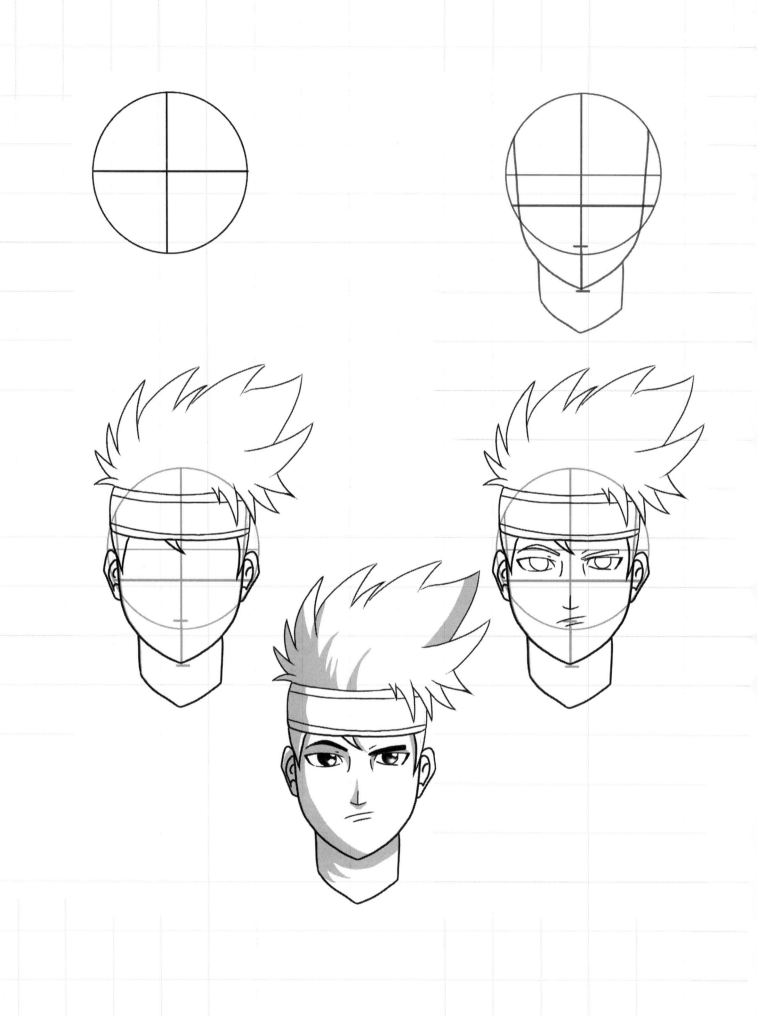

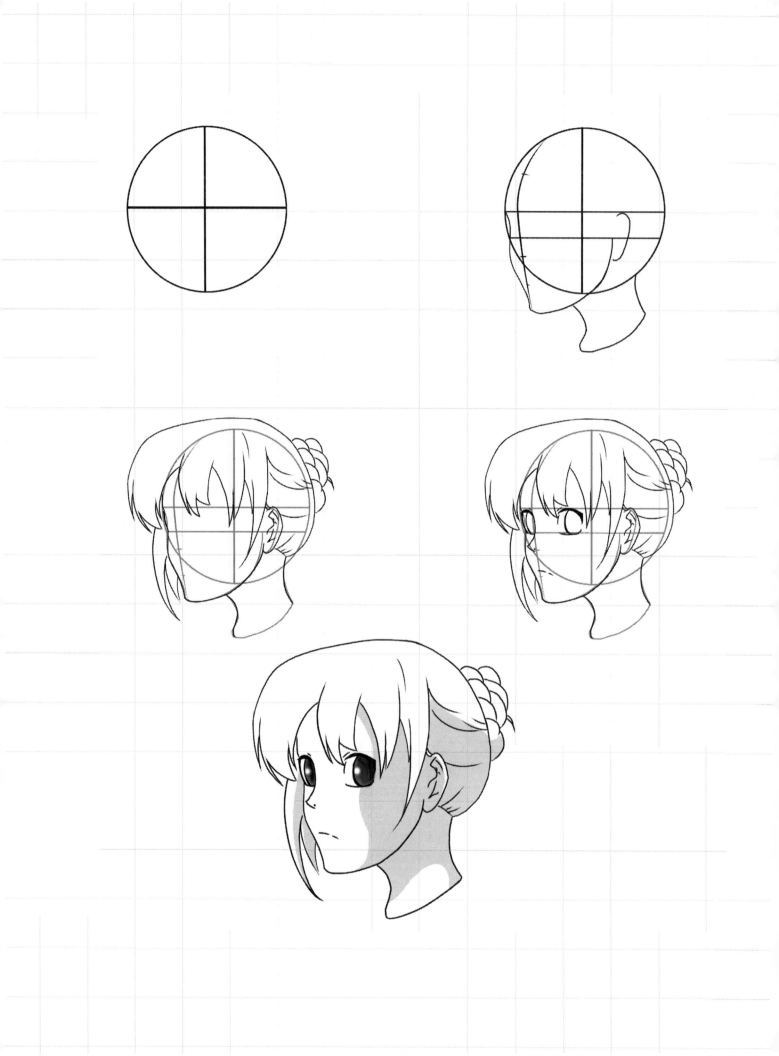

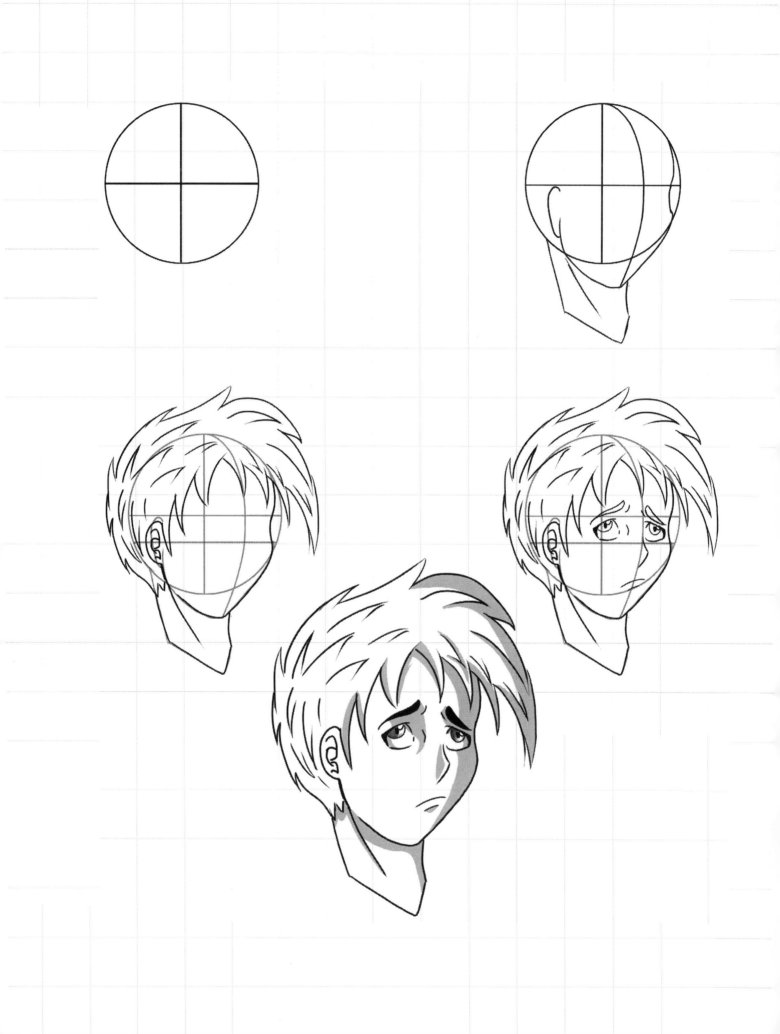

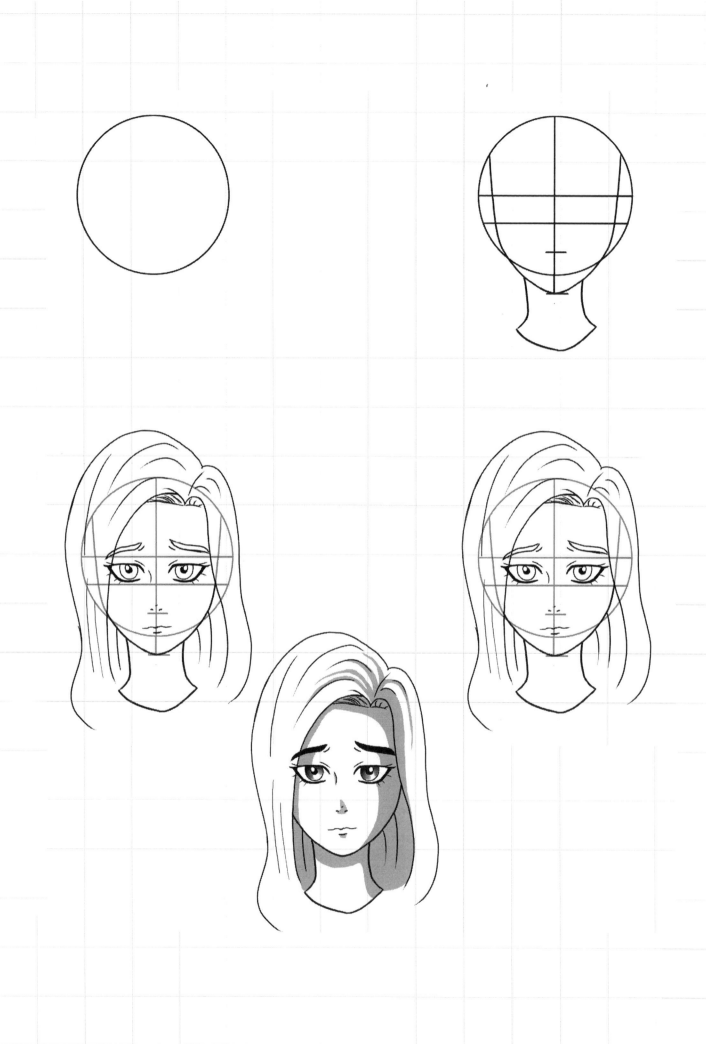

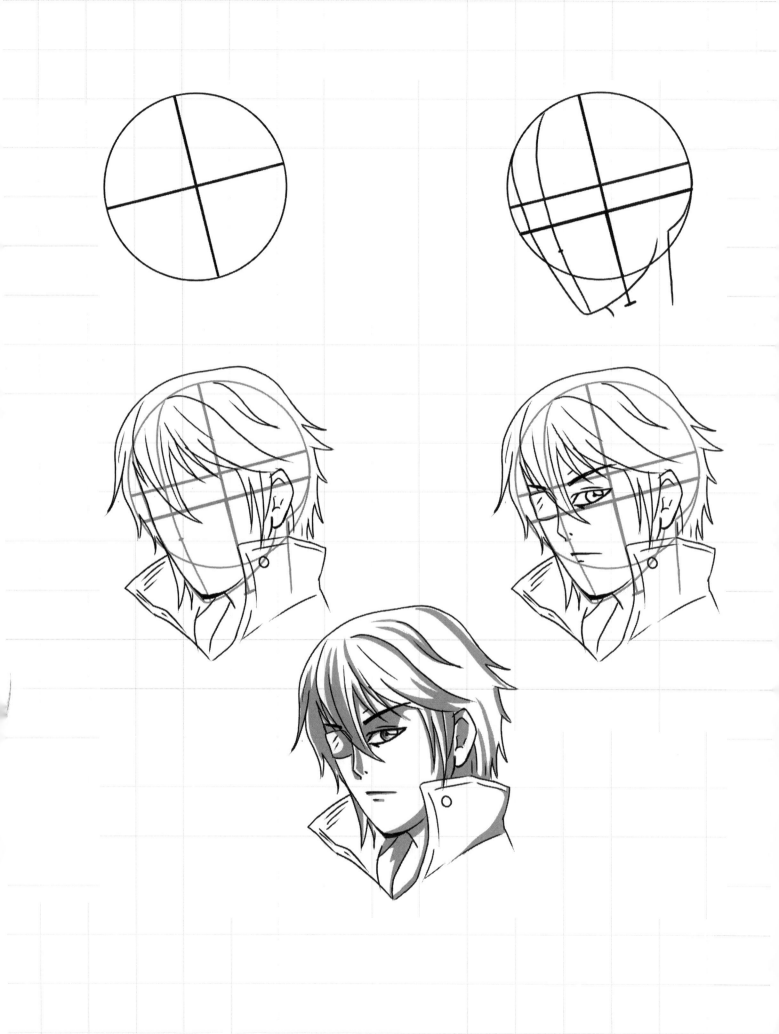

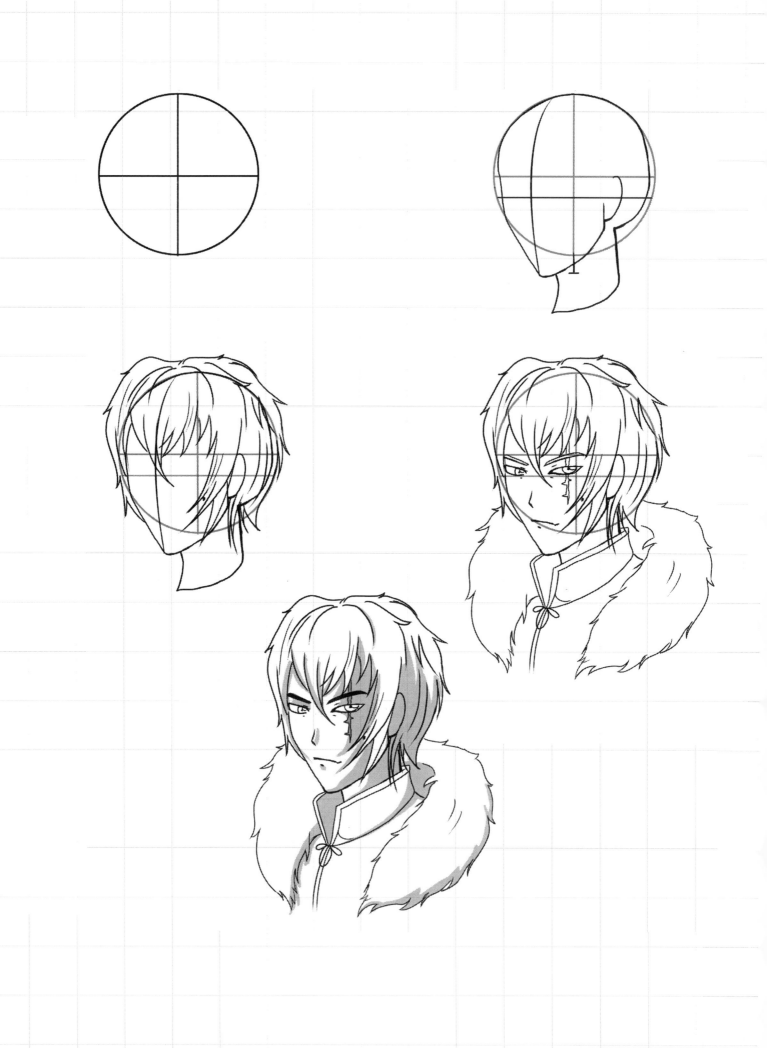

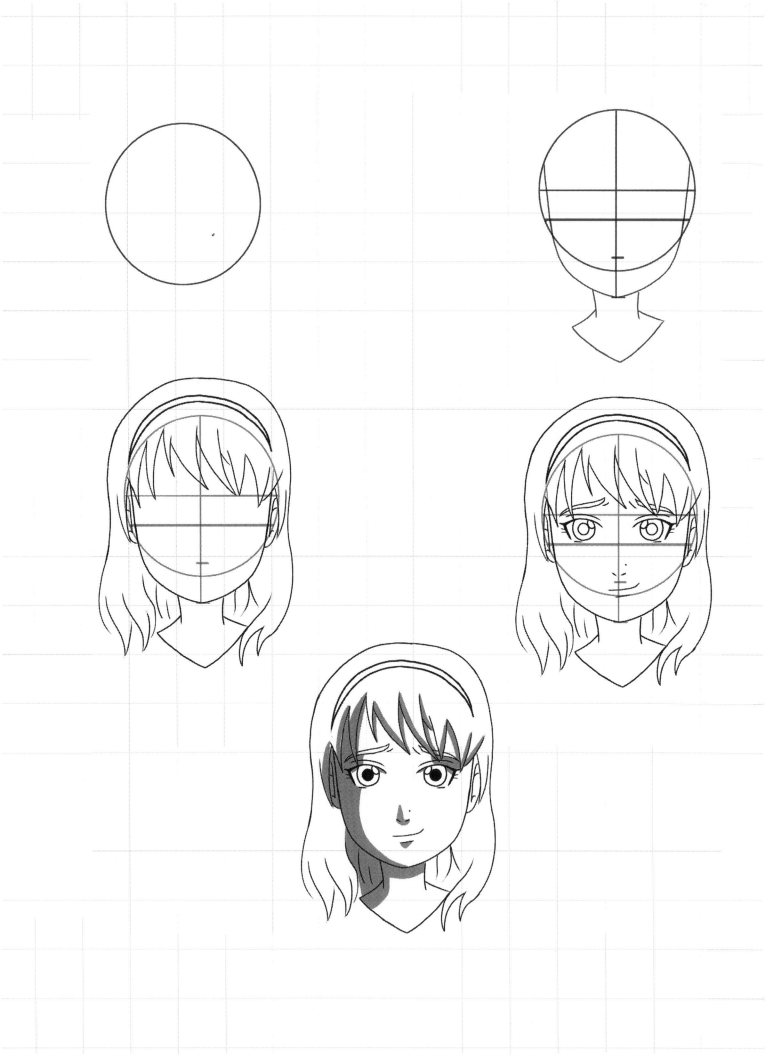

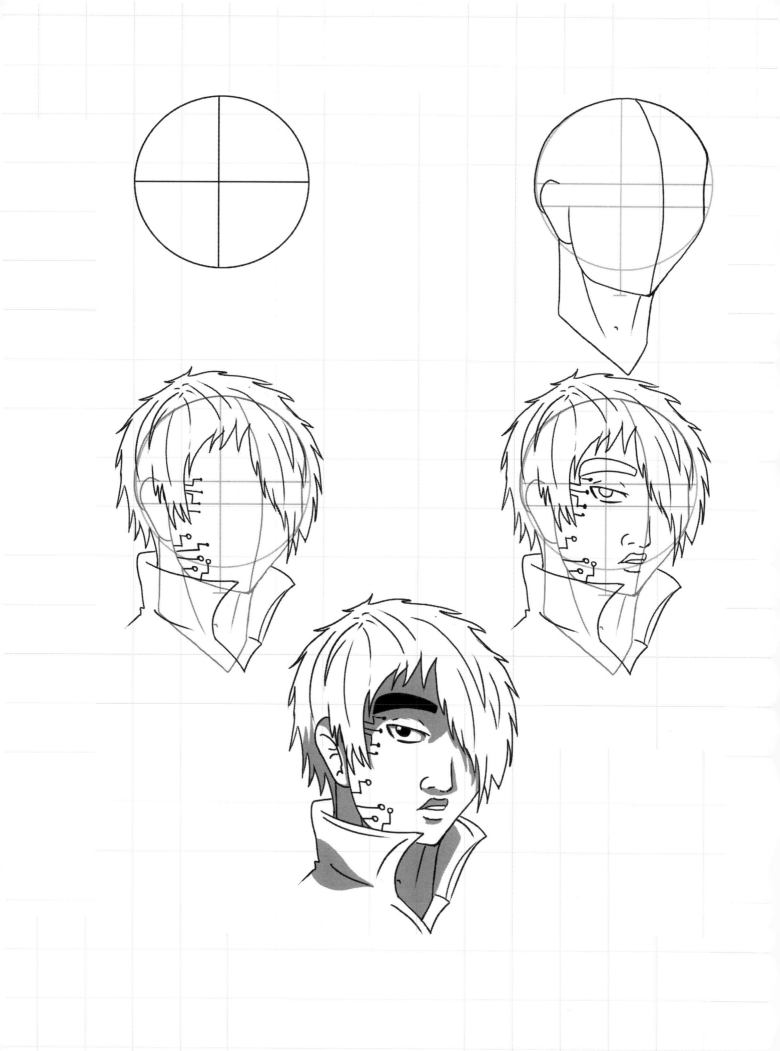

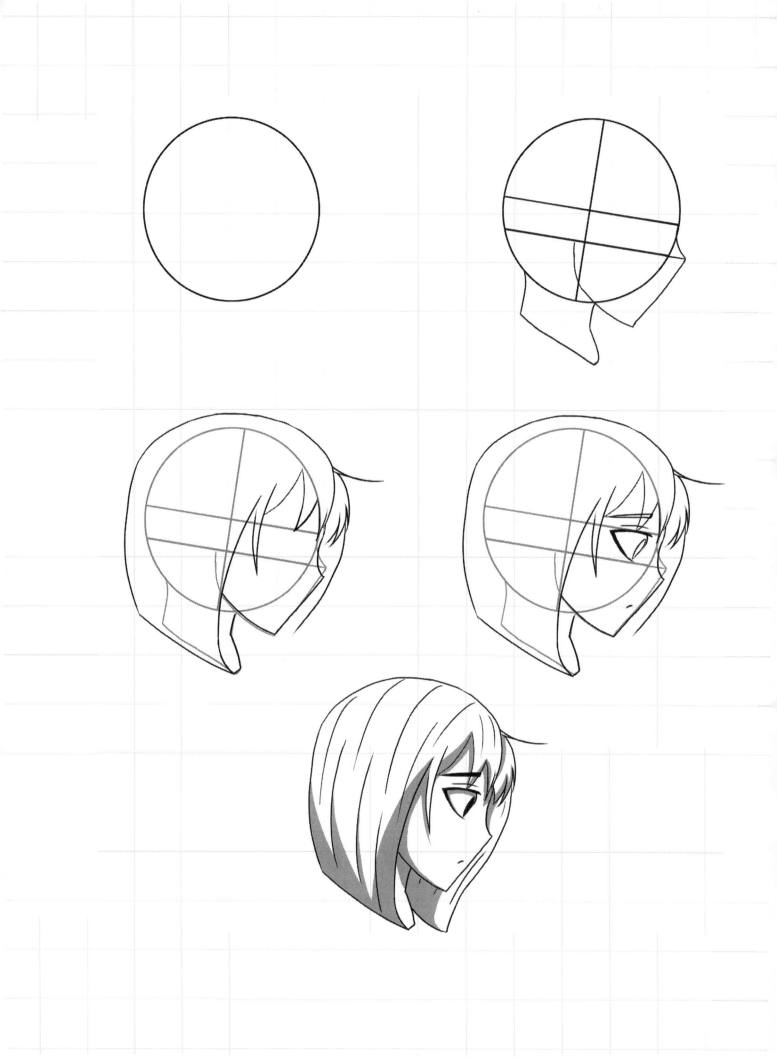

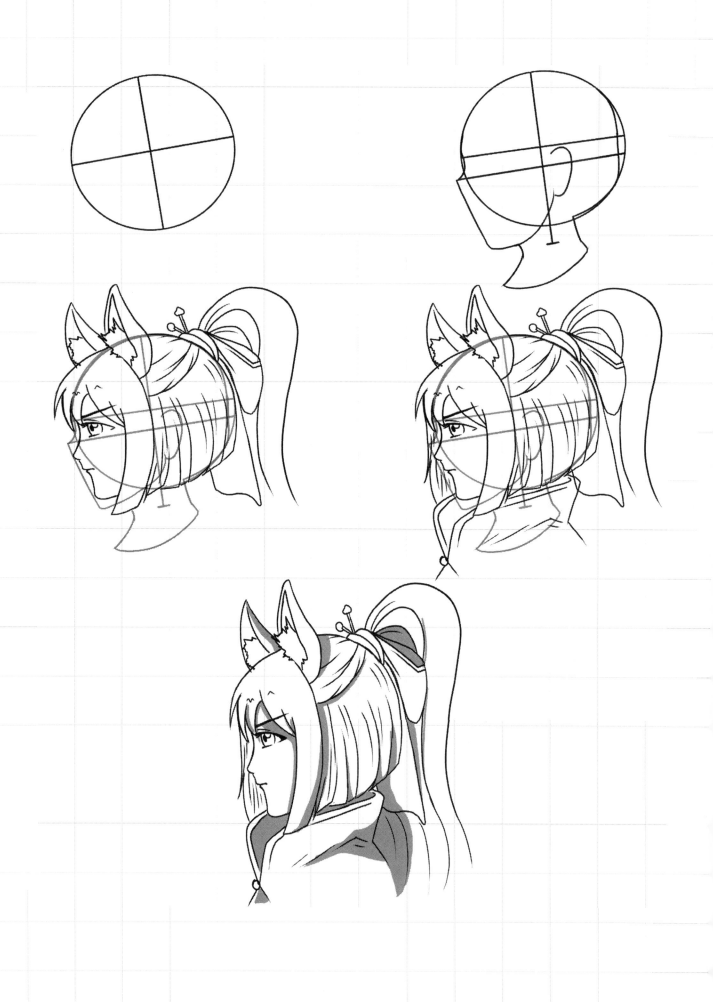

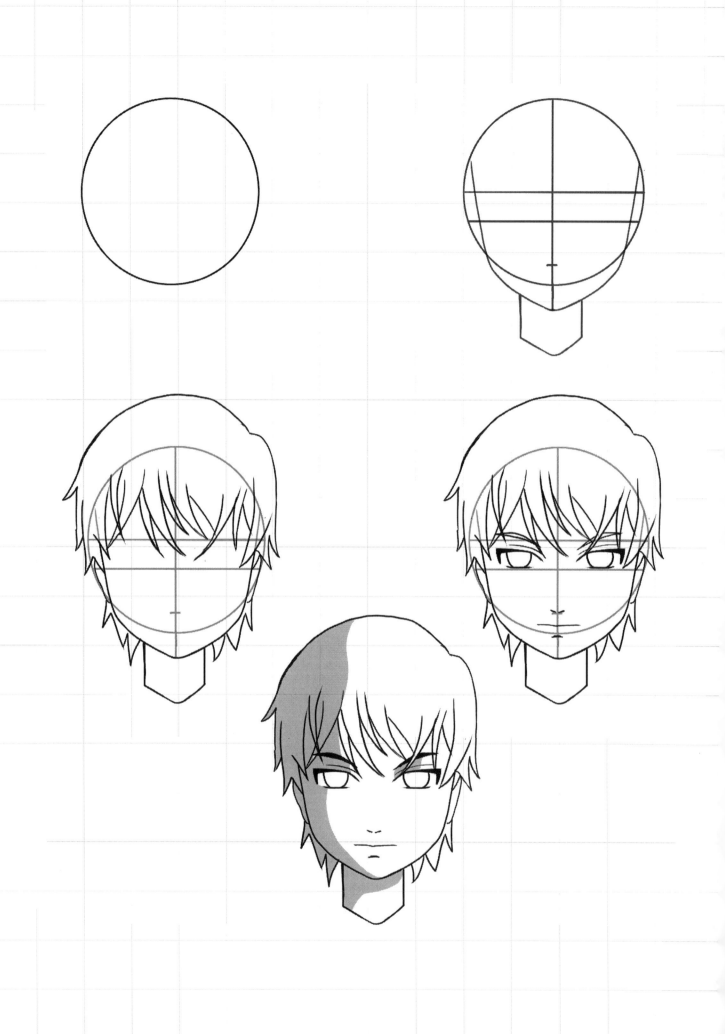

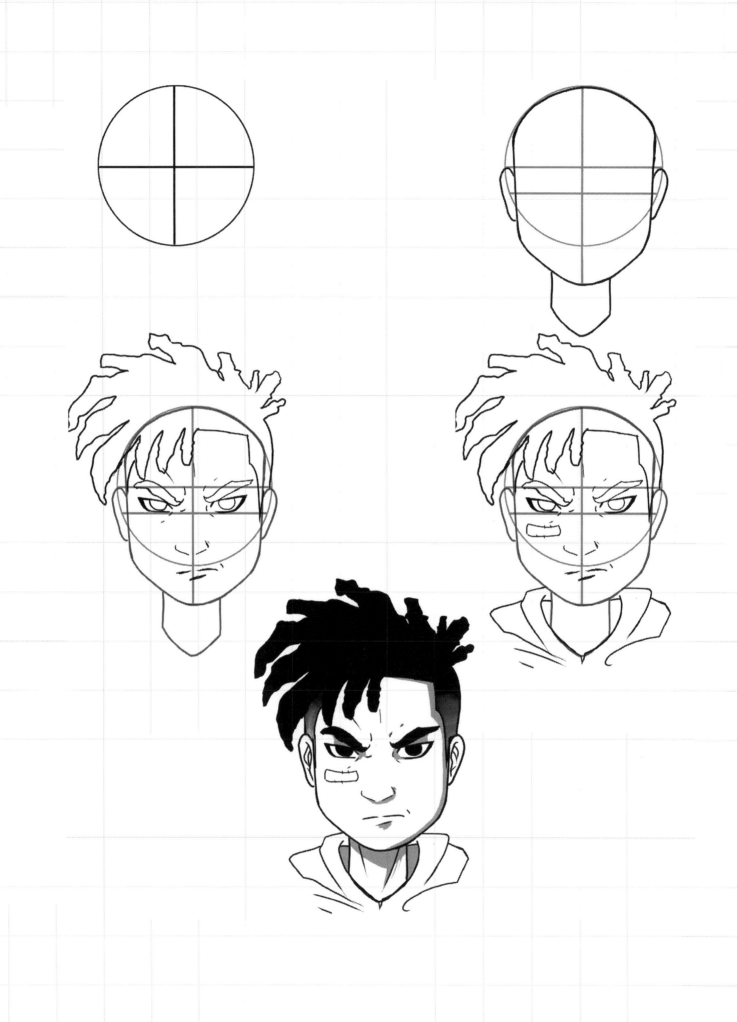

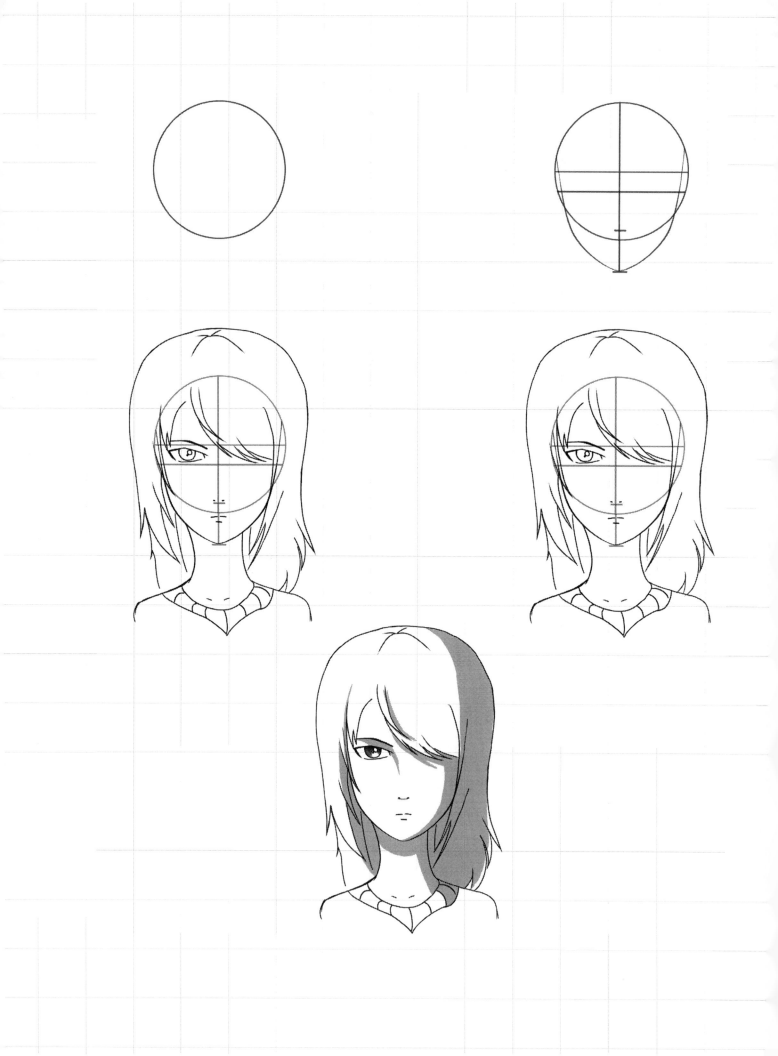

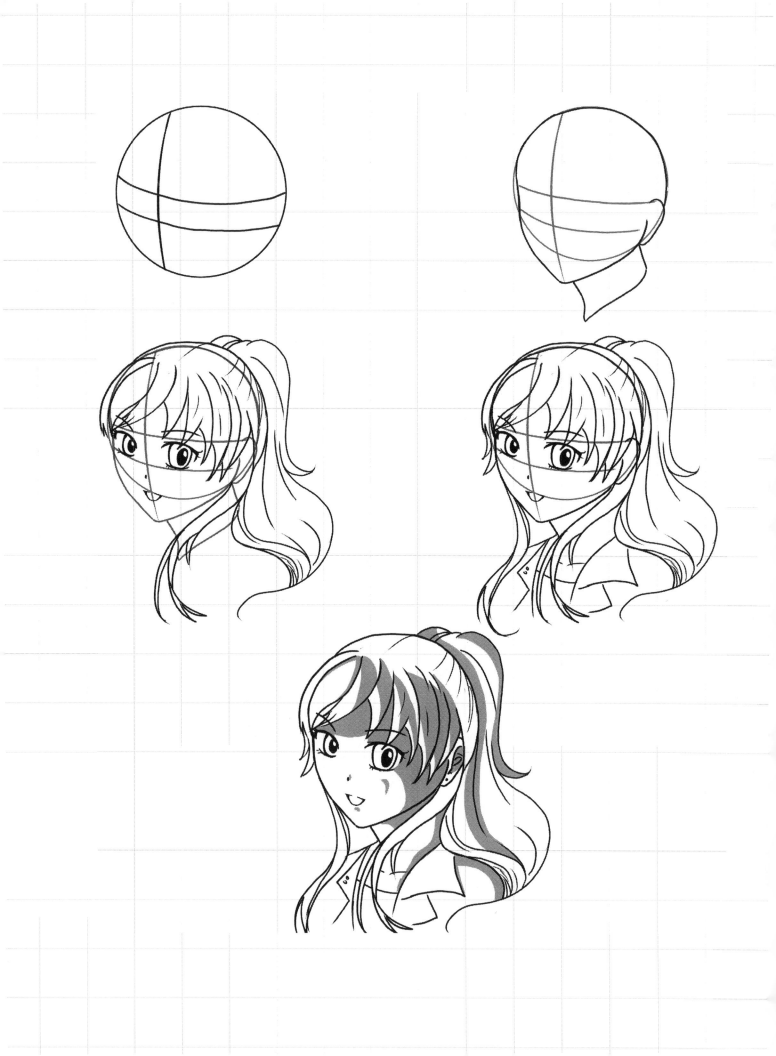

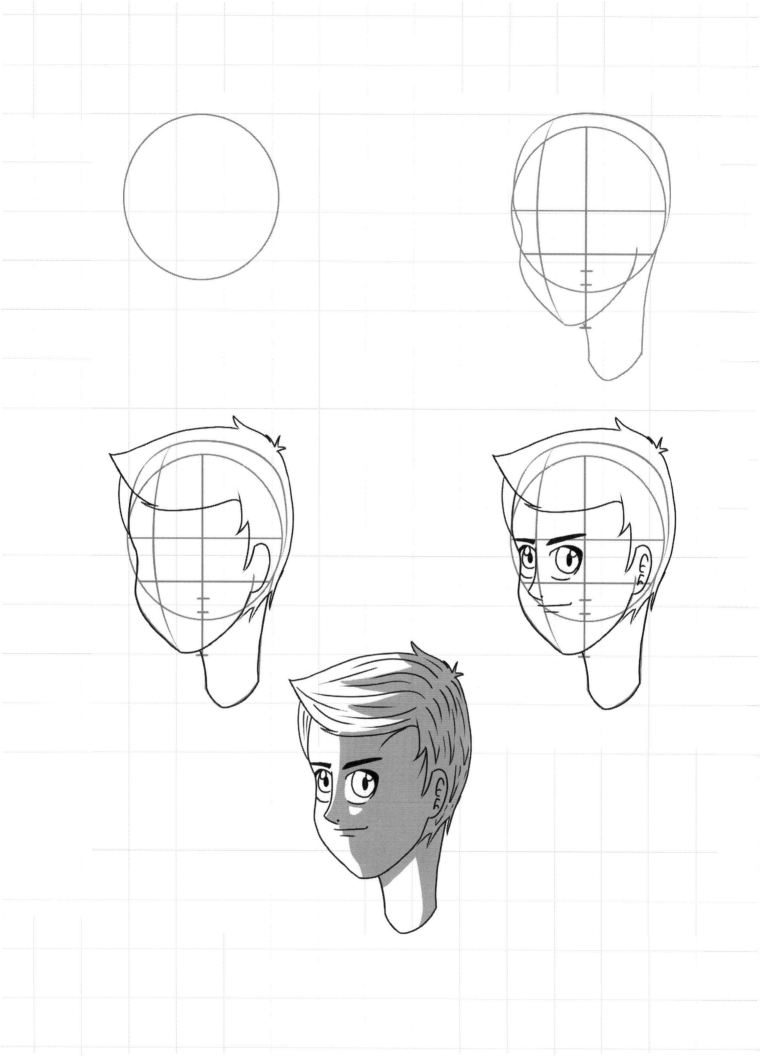

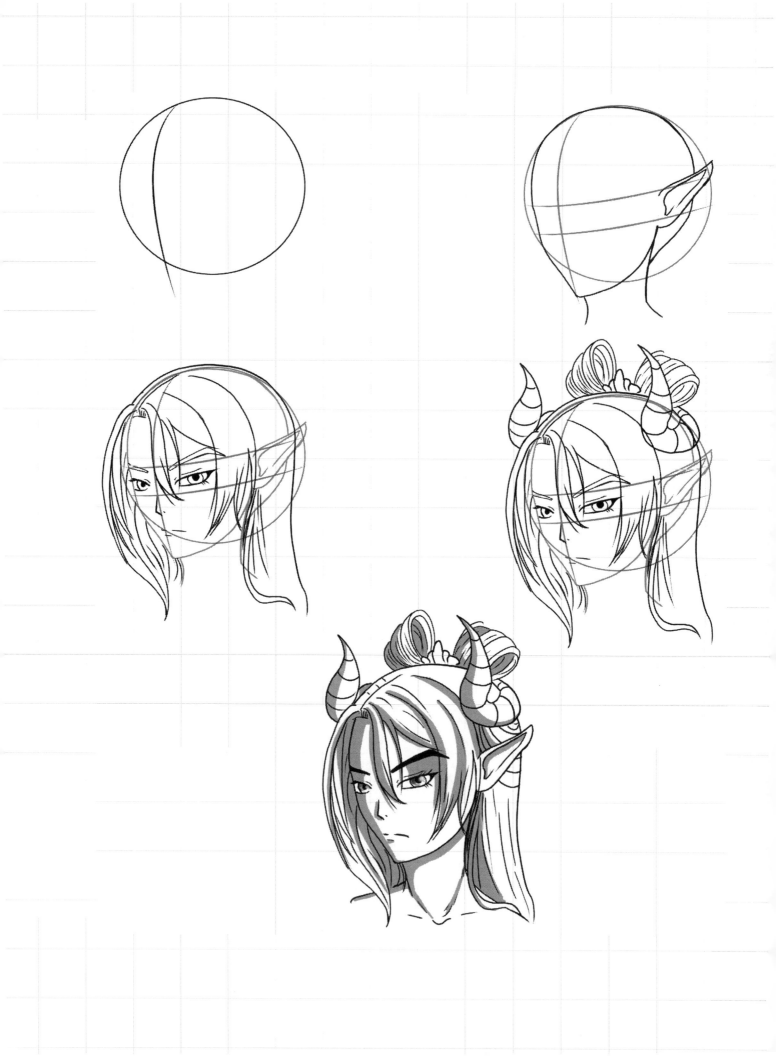

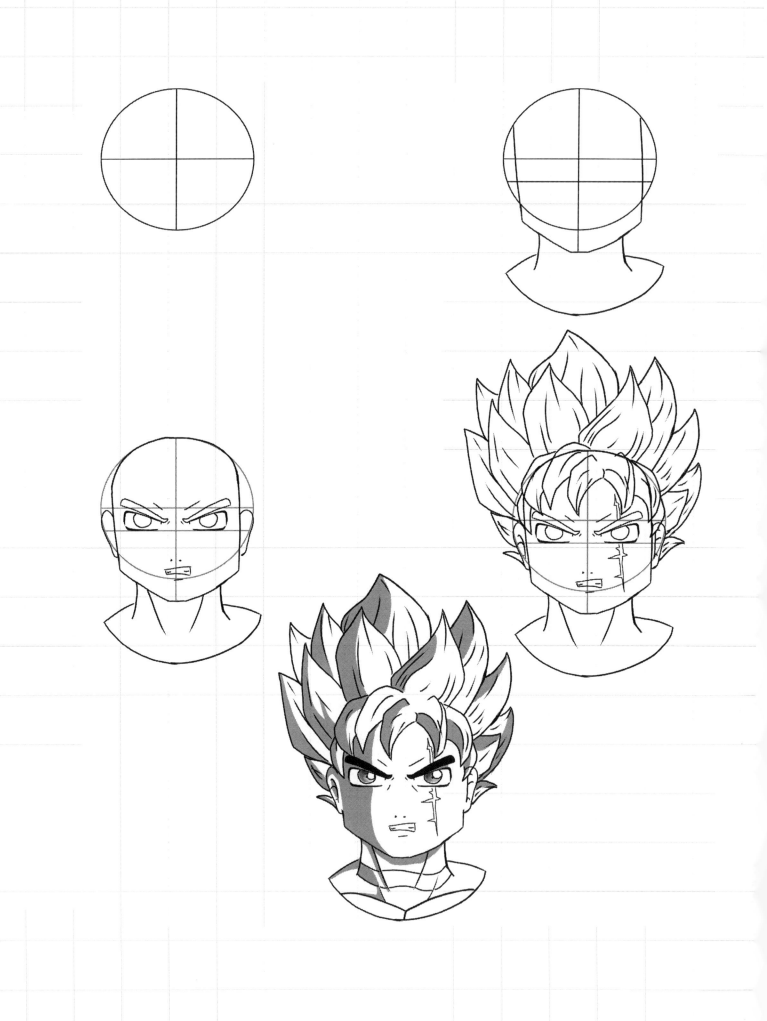

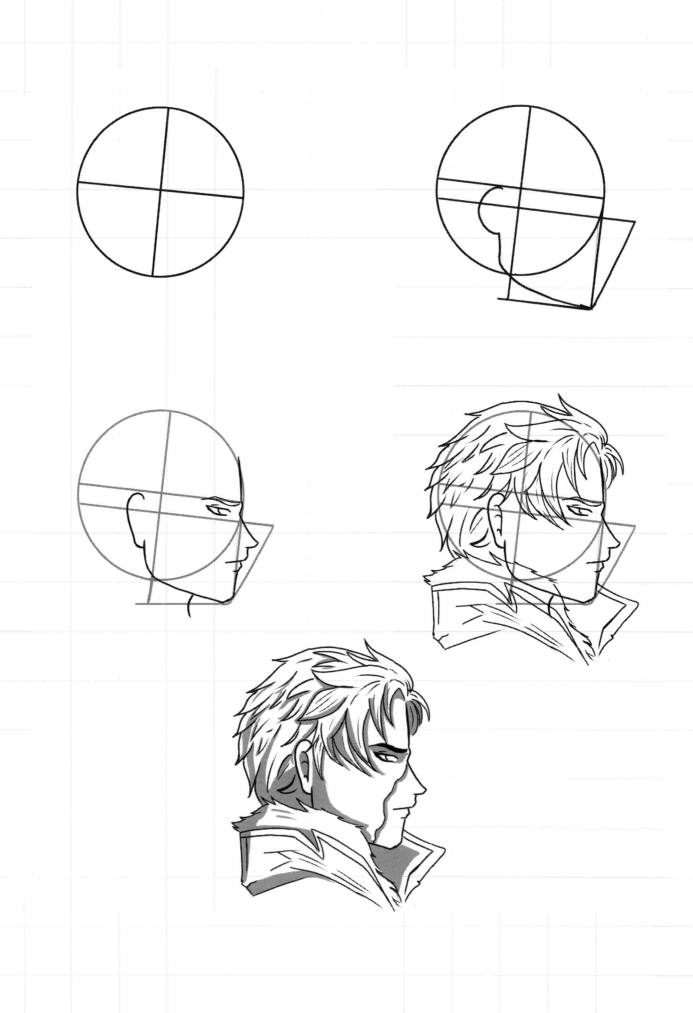

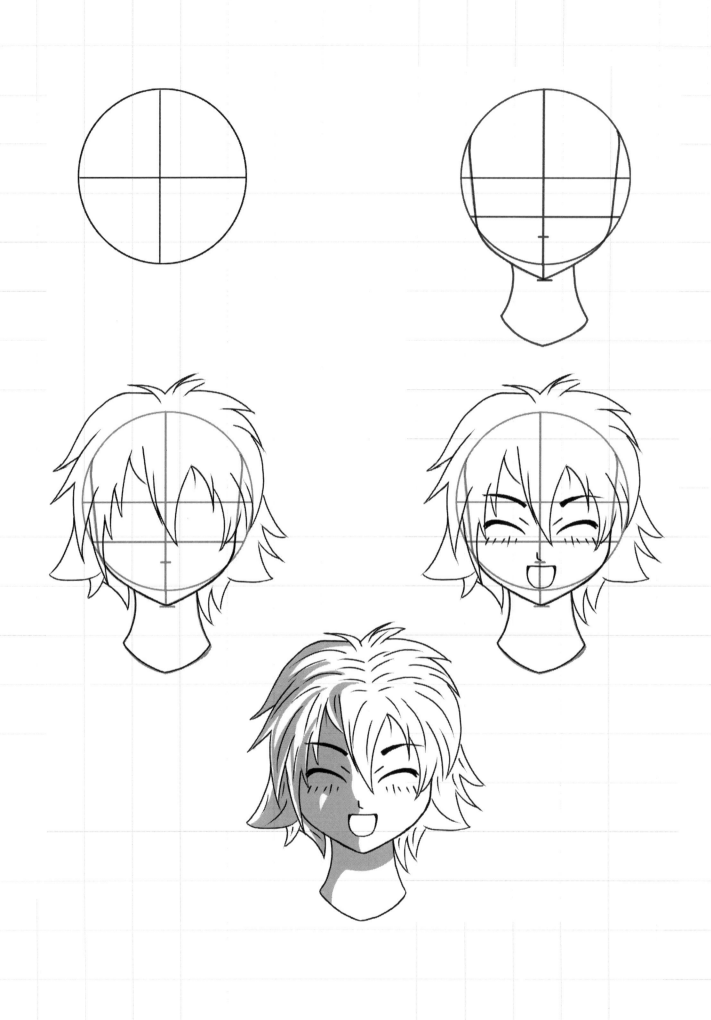

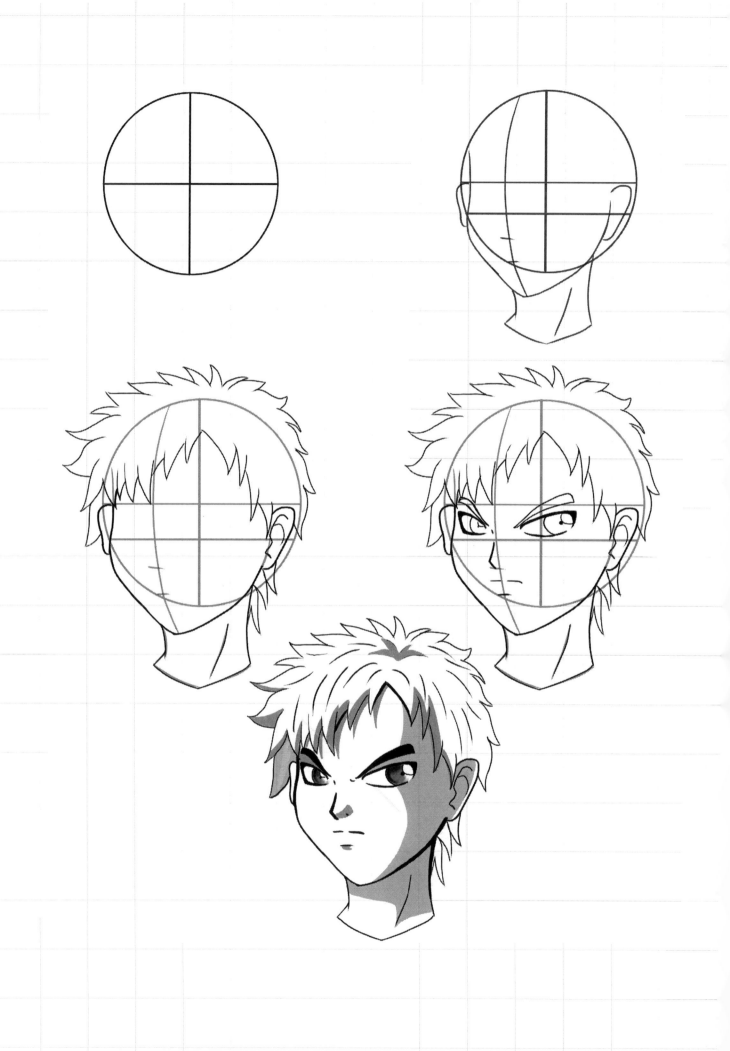

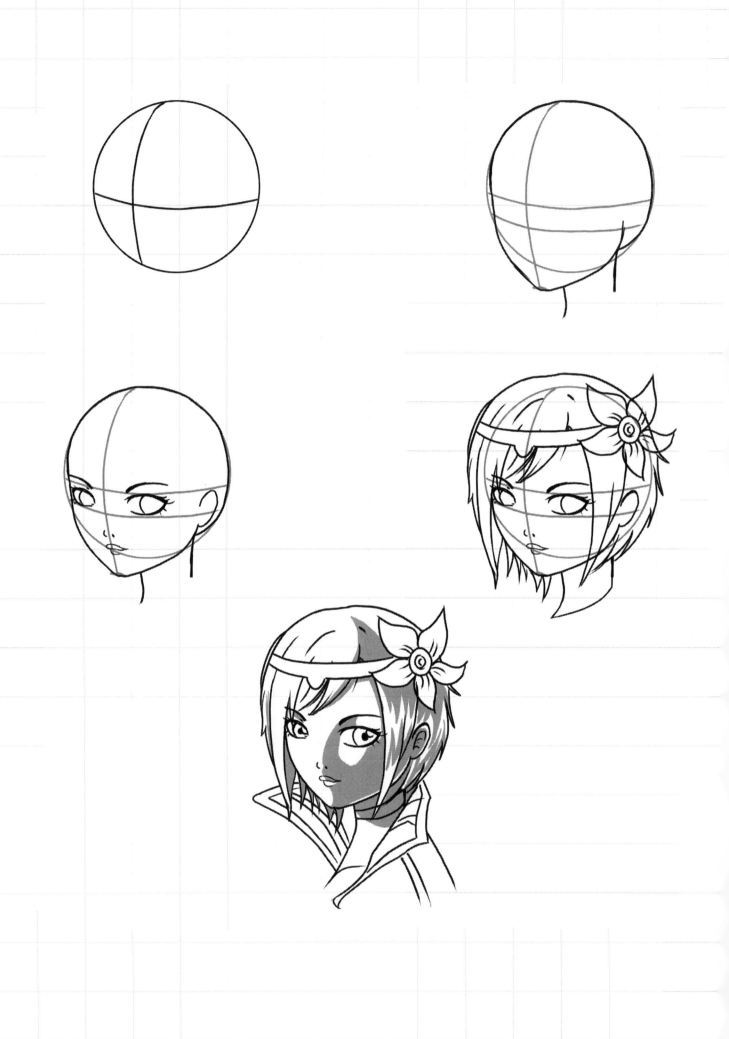

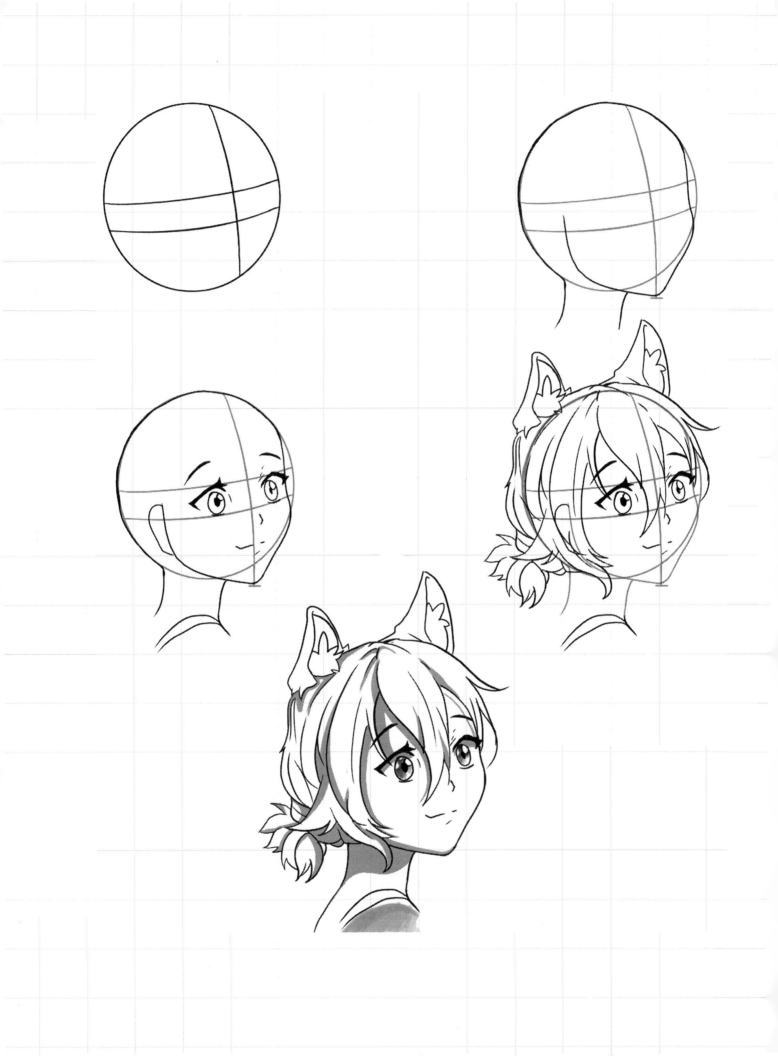

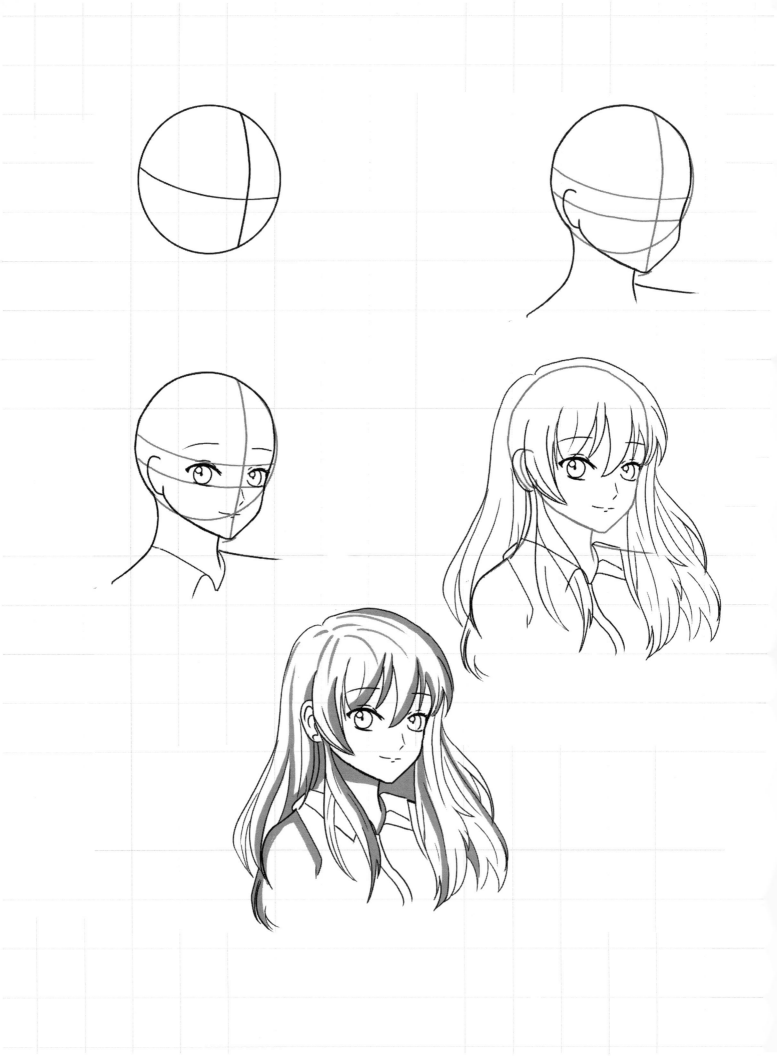

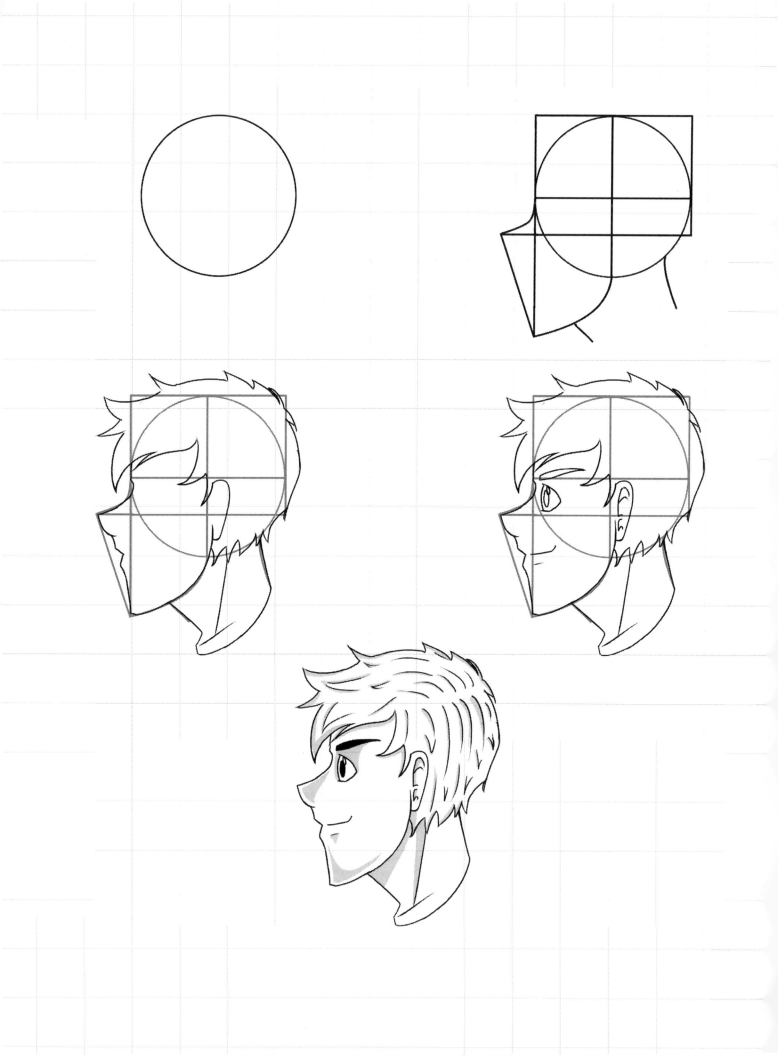

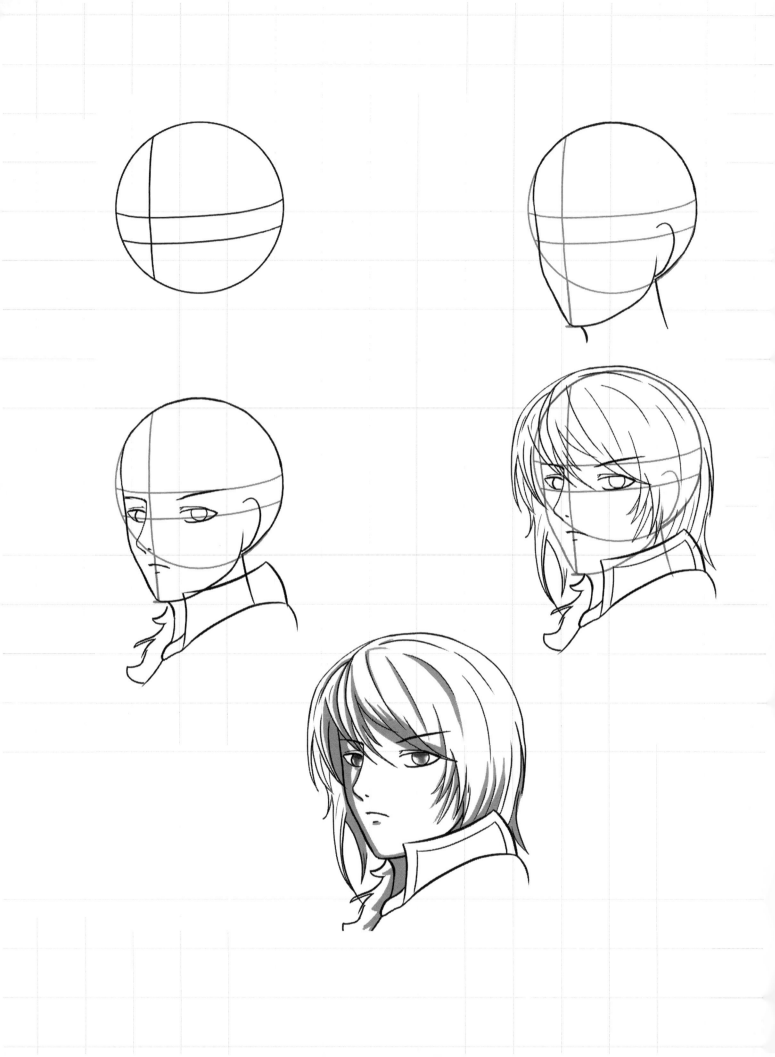

THANK YOU FOR YOUR PURCHASE!

We greatly appreciate your support. Without you, none of this would be possible. Please consider leaving us a review on Amazon.

Reviews greatly help us to be able to continue to produce books such as this one. Also, feel free to follow us on our social media channels or contact us directly at sketchpert.press@gmail.com

And be sure to join our exclusive Facebook Group for freebies, giveaways, and early preview copies!

@sketchperts

@sketchperts

Made in the USA
Las Vegas, NV
21 December 2020